Preparing My Daughter for Rain.

Key Ballah

ISBN: 1500233439
ISBN-13: 9781500233433

I wrote this for my future daughter.
I pray that the pain of this life,
never ever tightens your throat,
or hardens your heart.
It is better to be a pile of soft bones,
than a wall, made entirely of concrete.

- I love you.

5:105.

And to My Own Mother,
Heaven for me is at your feet.
And my heart has learned from yours
How to love as hard as it can.
I am grateful for all of the things
you've taught me,
and even though it seems like I always
wander off of the path you've drawn up
for me,
I keep you in my heart.
So, where ever my heart takes me,
where ever my God wills me
and where ever my feet decide to go,
you are there.
Forgive me for hurting you
all of the times my tongue was sharp.
I am a work in progress
and I am learning that your hands have
worn years of sacrifice,
that your back has carried my burdens
and yours,
and that you have never tried to lessen
that load.
Without you,
I wouldn't have learned how to fight.
Merci Mama,
Je t'aime.

The Body.

Your
body
is a gracious land,
show it mercy.
Always.

Collect
yourself
into your hands.
And give yourself
away,
like a gift.
Slowly
to the wind.
She loves you.

Call that story Being Free.

Your body wasn't made to be loved on
occasion.
It was made to be loved every night
with warm hands.
Every day with dedication,
in the same way that the sun goes to
bed every night, and rises in love
every morning.

Even if you gathered all of the
oceans into your throat, and all of the
light into your hair, there would still
be women who have mastered the art of
stealing stars out of the sky, and
hiding them in their eyes.
You are the kind of beautiful that
leaves craters in the moon,
the kind of beauty that has shaitans
banging at the gates of heaven, begging
God to let them have one last glimpse
of you.

Don't be concerned with other women's
beauty. Only admire God's amazing work
and wish them well, this earth was made
to bite us in half and grind us to
bone, but we were made to be kind.

Be kind to your body.
It will speak for you,
or against you one day.
Remember.

A Self-Love To Do List:

- Rinse your skin with warm water.
- Use your first finger on your right hand to eat honey out of the jar.
- Write yourself a love letter.
- Ask your mother to tell you how much she loves you. Listen carefully to the truth in her voice.
- Tell your father that you forgive him.
  (Try to forgive him, as cliché as it sounds, forgiveness really is for you).
- Read the first chapter of your favorite book, if you can't stop, read until you can.
- Go outside. No matter the weather, even if you just stand on a balcony, even if it's only for a few seconds. Fresh air buries sadness.
- Stretch..
- Touch all of your scars and remember their birthdays, remind yourself how far you've come.

Forgiveness is a weighty thing.
It is thick,
but spreads itself out thin,
like trying to love yourself,
with only a foggy memory of a time
when you knew what that looked like.
Forgive yourself,
stretch it across your skin,
let your forgiveness become you.

There are flowers growing from your
spine.
A garden, sprouting from your bones.
Evolved through revolution to end the
shame
that comes from laying on your back.

Do not allow your body to become a
civil war, it is almost impossible to
recover.
Ask your mother, she will tell you how
many years she's been fighting and how
many battles she's won.

You try to love your body,
but you can't seem to look at it with
both eyes open.
You want to appreciate your hands,
but it's hard to appreciate them when
they have contributed so foully to your
destruction.
These are your body politics,
it's okay to not trust yourself.
But eventually,
we all must heal.

Why does your nakedness offend you?
You were the inspiration for all of the
earth,
every rolling hill and rushing stream.
Land so beautiful,
they couldn't help but to steal it.

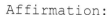

Affirmation:

    This body is brave even when I am
not.
Even when I am a puddle of sadness,
this body carries the weight well,
and I am no light being.

My body is accustomed to compromise.
I learned at a very young age how to
negotiate space.
How to apologize for the way that my
body fills all of the places that it
occupies and all of the places it
doesn't.
Teaching my body to grow free,
and wild,
and to not be afraid to exist,
has become my life's work.

You are an entity.
An important part of this universe.
A thread in a grand tapestry.
You are beautiful,
you are powerful,
you are here.
~~SubhanAllah.~~

My body is not a weapon that I was
meant to use against myself.
It is an intricate garden, who's
flowers remind me of God.

I pray you are never infected by the
insecurities that plagued your mother.
Or the late night devastation that
comes from not loving even a sliver of
yourself.
I pray that you never wake up in the
morning, with loneliness waiting for
you at the foot of your bed.
I promise he is no companion.
I pray I can teach you the value of
your body, the value of your heart.
I pray that you never find yourself
kneeling in front of a toilet, with two
fingers pressed down into the back of
your tongue, trying to paint the toilet
bowl in your self-loathing.
It is a colour that is unbecoming, even
on you.
I pray that I can teach you that beauty
is subjective; this is something I
didn't begin to understand until I was
at least twenty.
I pray most of all, that you learn how
important fajr is. And how truly
blessed you are to be a woman.

Have you ever looked at your body
without the lens of your colonized
mind?

Hating my stretch marks
and my bicycle wounds
and breasts that are victim to gravity,
or life.
Legs that have had to run from people
they've trusted.
Hands that have had to hold themselves,
Leaving change rooms behind in a river
of tears,
leaving lovers waist deep in my
insecurities,
pretending to be confident,
not being able to look at myself naked,
not being able to look at myself
clothed,
comparing myself to my sister,
wishing my hair was longer and
straighter,
wishing my skin was lighter,
wishing I was someone else,
asking God to make me beautiful.
These are things I beg my daughter not
to inherit.

Your body wasn't made to be consumed
by greedy men, with no understanding of
your value. You are worth infinity, do
you understand?

The Heart.

I have forgotten,
after all of the heartbreak and bad
decisions,
to thank my heart for not giving up.
To thank it for fighting for me,
because I know that it's tired
so tired.

When you can't stop thinking about him,
and you know that you have to,
when you burn at thoughts of him,
when you wait by your phone for him,
when he consumes you.
When you have no memories except for
the ones he's in,
  When you ask God to save you,
but instead he says "swim".
When your skin feels tight, and every
waking minute makes you nauseous.
Remember, that your grandmother
survived,
she lived through the love,
she weathered the thick black of the
storm,
it took her years,
but she did it.
And you Queen, were cut from the same
cloth.

I loved even the ugly parts in you,
the parts that made me gag and spit and
cringe.
I saw myself in those parts,
and I couldn't look away.

...and I've waited too long
for men who've wanted nothing more than
a warm body.
I've waited with emptying hands, aching
heart, and ill advised "wisdom" from
aunties who tell me that my body is
only a sanctuary, a temple that I
myself may never enter.
Sometimes I want to be desecrated in a
way that makes me feel alive,
sometimes I want to spend the rest of
my life in prostration,
forgetting just how ugly their dirty
hands have made me feel.

I've looked everywhere for you, even
in spaces and times that no longer
exist. I traveled to the edge of the
earth, and beat on the doors of heaven
to see if maybe God had saved you from
this place. And my feet hurt, and my
back aches and I have grown accustomed
to walking days without water, because
I know when I find you I will have my
fill. For you I am a Nomad.

I wanted you,
in every way someone shouldn't want
someone else.
In every way that God begs you not to.
The kind of wanting that your parents
lock you away for.
The kind of wanting that leaves your
mother bawling and crying on the floor
of the foyer of your house,
at 3:30 in the morning,
slapping her chest and pounding the
ground,
beseeching God, asking him why he gave
her a daughter like you
after you come home covered in finger
prints,
that look strikingly like the devils.

You will have lovers who will love you
with full passionate hearts.
Intact hearts and sound minds.
You will also have lovers who plunge
into you, smashing their hearts against
you like waves striking rocks.
They will break themselves open
into pieces so small they will glitter
in the sun.
You will have lovers who will love you
by standing next to you,
and others who love you out of a pile
of dust.
Remember, that either way,
you will be loved,
you are loved.

Some men don't know what it means to
stay.
They've watched their mothers leave
every morning,
and their fathers leave every night.
We think, maybe that's where they
learned their disappearing act.
But I know women who've lived their
entire lives in empty homes,
and the absence has taught them
something else.

It's been almost five years,

and I still miss the way that you would
call me in the middle of the night
to tell me that your hands were
whispering my name,
and how your lips were missing my
mouth,
and how your ears were craving my
voice,
and that
there was no way that you could wait
until the morning
to tell me how much you loved me.
Your memory lives on me
like an old scar, in a place that only
I know,
with a story that only I find
beautiful.

Days are days,
and nights are nights.
But when you are gone,
everythingmeltstogether.
And one hour feels like
a thousand years of loneliness.

When he touches you like you are the
last person he will ever touch.
When he runs you through his fingers
with every bit of tenderness he can
flesh out of his bones.
When he says your name like tidal waves
and kisses you like a midnight in July.
Hold him close,
project your thanks to the heavens,
and find what you've been waiting for
in the closeness of your skin.

I want you to love me so deeply,
that the sky cracks herself open out of
jealousy, begging you to turn your eyes
back to her.

25 Questions to ask before falling in
love:

1. Do you still hold your mother's
hand?
2. Do sun rises inspire you?
3. Do you believe in God?
4. Do you like being touched?
5. What will you name your daughter?
6. Where is heaven? Does it exist?
7. How many cracks are there in your
spine?
9. How essential is the rain for your
soul?
10. Would you kill for someone you
love?
11. Have you ever been in love? Why did
you stop?
12. Did you ever see your father kiss
your mother?
13. What was/is your great grandmothers
name?
14. Do you miss your country?
15. Where are your boarders?
16. What is your favorite word?
17. Have you ever held a gun?
18. Do you know what salt water smells
like?
19. What does forever mean to you?
20.Have you ever broken a bone?
21.What was the ugliest thing in your
childhood home?
22. Do you like the way it feels to
push down on a bruise?
23. How important is Kindness to you?
24. Is this life satisfying?
25. Could you love me?

I am a garden for your blood,
a safe place for your lineage.
A house for your trinity.

His hands were old,
And not in a beautiful way,
in the same way that makes the snow
grey,
the same dirty old, that governs empty,
littered chip bags.
There was a certain filth to his hands,
the kind that no one could scrub out.
And I knew all of this
even before he touched me,
even before he cornered me and asked
if I had ever loved a man,
even before I lied and said yes,
because I thought at 18,
women should already be stained by
love.

It's 3:45 am
and I woke up because I had
a dream that my skin was separating
around my bones.
It takes a while for my eyes to adjust
in the dark, but now that I'm awake, I
hear the rain pelting the house,
threatening to crack it in half, my
head is pounding trying to split itself
in two, the lightening is trying to
break this world open to let the purity
of the heavens through, the moon is
crying she is missing her other half.
All of this chaos, and only on night
one of missing you.

I am tired,
and I want to sleep,
but your memory
sprawls out
in every place I choose to lay.

I gargle sea water in an attempt to
burn you out of my throat.
But every time I go to speak, your name
still falls out into hands that have
dried waiting for you.

Our garden has withered where it once
grew free,
our love has withered where it once
grew wild.
I have withered from the thickness of
it all,
and all of this loss has made me
hungry.

I prayed,
and you came,
like a plethora of suns.
Like a sky full of moons,
and a mouth full of well wishes.
Like hands full of warmth,
and a heart that has ached for a
century,
finally finding love.
You came as a result of my asking,
as a result of midnight prayer,
and midday begging.
As a result of red hot skin
and puffy eyes.
You are so much good,
birthed from years of sadness.
You are a proof that God exists.

David slayed Goliath with a single
stone.
You crippled my heart with a single
lie.
This is the enormity of small things.

When I love,
the moons stops
in the middle of the sky,
and my heart prepares the rest of my
body for
war.

I only ever asked him
to love me deeply
and earnestly,
but he still turned around
and said,
that I was too heavy,
that I was asking too much,
that he was only one man.
After him I learned,
that sometimes,
it takes two men to do,
the work of one woman.

I don't dream of you anymore,
I am a refugee in someone else's
country now.

The bible says,
that Eve's sin was punished by pain in
child birth.
But the older I get and the more that I
see,
It has become clear to me that Eve's
punishment wasn't the pain,
her punishment was Adam himself.

I knew that the danger would make me
fall in love with him.
I am a magnet for men with intentions
made of straw.
A flame, that sets fire to every
sunrise
but cuts herself open as a sacrifice
for it's setting.
Did you know that women who bleed fire,
become black widows for men whose hands
haven't been washed since the last body
they painted red?
When I looked at you I knew that you
could be my undoing,
and so I opened my arms and welcomed
you home.

I was swollen.
A brick house of a woman.
A dying leaf hanging half off of a
rotting tree.
Pregnant with poisonous love for you,
and tragically miscarrying myself.
You asked me to bend,
so I bent 'til I snapped.
a contortionist for love.
I split, down the middle,
right in half like the temple veil.
No rabbi, no priest, no knowledge.
Just a woman giving birth
to her still born self,
and a man who liked to watch her burn
for him.

There are some men, who can call you
out of the blue in the middle of the
night, and make you forget every
promise you've ever made to yourself.

Those men are dangerous, run.

When I have a daughter I will tell her
You grew between the cracks of my skin,
I built you,
cell by cell,
over nine full moons,
a flower grown from blood.
Somewhere in your beautiful mind lives
the distant memory, of loving only the
sound of my voice and the slow hammer
of my heart,
you trusted me before you knew me.
So if you ever question your capability
to love fully, remember you have loved
before, and you will love again

Ask him why he can't commit.
Ask him.
Ask him how he can say he loves you but
not check on you everyday.
Why he can call you in the middle of
the night but not first thing in the
morning.
Why he can't say your name without
splintering his tongue.
Ask him where he goes after he leaves
you.
Who he's with when he says he's at
home.
Tell him you don't trust him.
Tell him that he makes you crazy,
that his half ass'd attempts at
security drive you mad.
Tell him.
Tell him that you don't like the way
that loving him makes you feel, that
you wake up every morning aching.
Tell him, you hurt more, you sleep less
and it always feels like you are too
weighty for him.
Ask him why he can't commit,
why he leaves and returns just when you
think you can live without him.
Ask him why he can't stay,
Why he's committed to leaving but not
committed to you.
Ask him why you never feel like you can
ask him these things?
Why he gets to live weightless,
while you live shoulder deep inside
him.

Your heart,
has never stopped beating for you.
Even after him,
even after her,
in all of the loss,
in all of the clawing away at yourself.
It stayed loyal
it loved you,
when you didn't love yourself.

The Land.

The ships came,
and turned the oceans to blood.
Maybe that is where our
fear of the water came from.

Once I was an African,
but now I am told to run before the
word stains my skin.
They say: "Tell me everything else, but
don't tell me that"
So when they ask me where I'm from,
I say here, and point to this blood
stained earth.
When they ask what I'm mixed with, I
explain the intricate strings of my
existence.
I tell them about the boat, but never
the anchor.
When they touch my hair and eat my
skin,
I tell them every place that my
ancestors walked from,
but I never say Africa.
India, France, St.Vincent, insert
ethnic mix here, hide the entire
continent in the folds of your tongue.
They've taught me to be ashamed of
falling flesh, too afraid to remember
how easy it is to be stolen.
They make us run and say look how fast
they are,
they laugh because once upon a time we
weren't fast enough.
We are blatant with our self-hate,
every time they ask us where,
we jump at the chance to say every
place our limbs have brushed
but forget to tell them where our blood
was born.

For my daughter,
I want to draw our family tree,
on the soles of your feet.
that way you will have roots
where ever you choose to go.

My mother named me the same way they
name hurricanes,
something gentle on the tongue and
dangerous to the heart.

This land is not sweet,
because it is not mine.
But my land is sweet,
wherever it is,
sometimes I smell it on the wind,
and hear it in a dream,
she says she remembers me.
Today that is enough.

We were dried bodies digging in the
sand
for our mothers lost at sea.
Too afraid of the water to learn how to
swim,
The Ghosts were beckoning.
We listened from the shore,
they begged us to save them from the
water,
they pleaded with us to take them home.
But we were too afraid to tell them
that we don't know
where home is.

I carry in my mouth,
all of the words that my mother never
got a chance to speak into me.
All of the anger that the blackness of
my father's skin affords him.
The sea sick of my ancestors.
Laced into the seams of my tongue are
days of cotton mouthed prayer,
begging a silent God in secret.
Bloody thighs, coarse hair.
My mouth is a grave yard.
It is where I carry revolution,
thousands of brown fists, oceans of
carnage and spilled limbs.
Between the slight of my incisors lives
contradiction mixed into broken syntax.
My mouth is an infinite garden.
Plant your seeds in my gums,
I will speak you into fruition,
I, the goddess of unwavering savagery.
Merciless and capable,
will dance on the graves of my
oppressors.
To a long forgotten slave song with war
drums.
I will lead an exodus with my lips,
and soothe the hearts of my lovers with
my tongue.
I will never cry wolf,
trust me.

The sea
stood still
and wept for you.
Not angry and loud,
but calmly and quietly thanking you for
coming home.

There is a place in Africa,
with my memory sprouting from the
ground.
A place where I was thought of before I
was even imagined.
A place where my name is something
else
and my bones are at rest.
A place where my blood is still smeared
in sand,
a place I will never know,
even though I try to,
because,
when you are stolen
you are forced to forget,
even if the earth hasn't.

I was made during a gathering.
A thousand calloused hands picking and
sorting,
mashing and pounding,
low humming and hunting foot.
Barefooted children hanging off of full
breast.
I was made in a language forgotten by
colonized tongue,
by feet that scare the devil,
Bannok and fried plantain,
sweat lodge and Vincentian sun.
I was made in a gathering place,
by a thousand gathering hands rubbing
womb,
breathing into it one story.

You are home wherever you decide to be,
they stole your body and your land, but
you were not stolen,
you were always free.

The Soul.

When the sky opens
and God is waiting in the tide,
I will go to the ocean
And drink until I drown,
or until I die of thirst,
whichever comes first.

How do you tempt the moon out of the
sky into your hands?
You ask her to stay
and then let her choose
between you
and the vastness of space.

When I die,
do not cremate me.
Let my mother and sisters wash me, wrap
me in a white sheet
and send me home.
Remember that I loved fearlessly
with everything bleeding wildly,
Remember that I learned not to
apologize for my fire.

Evidences of God:

The motion of the sea,
The green of the landscape,
The blood of my daughter's womanhood.
The dying of my own womb,
The ripping of thunder,
The pressing of the rain,
The weight of my breasts,
The ache in my back,
The arch in my feet,
My grandmother's first name,
The colour of my skin,
The heat of my country,
The way that I worship.
My Heart,
The morning after love,
Dying trees,
Empty bellies,
The thickness of time,
Wandering eyes,
Broken promises,
Today,
Today,
Today.

10 Things I've Learned About
Forgiveness:

1. Forgive every inch of yourself.
Every inch. Even the places on you that
were left behind by greedy boys.
2. When you can't cry and your body is
begging you to soften, remember the way
your mother fought for you. Remember
her tears, remember her stiff chest,
and every blow she took from your
fathers whipping tongue.
3. Kiss your own hands. Don't be angry
at yourself for men who could never be
gentle with their own fingers.
4.When someone tells you that you're
emotional, thank them. Thank them for
recognizing the part in you that
recognizes God.
5. Drink water, your body will always
accept that apology.
6. You will never (fully) forget.
7. Healing is Divine. Accept it
gracefully.
8.Forgive yourself for being weak
beneath the weight of him, he is a man
who carries 4 generations of baggage.
9.The morning brings a new day, new
opportunities to be forgiven.
10. Growing bitterness inside of you,
will only turn you into a field of
sadness.

If you ever turn around and find that
it has been 3 months since you've faced
Makkah,
and your shame is so over whelming that
it crashes over you like a tidal wave,
DO NOT RUN.
Let that disgust wash over you
and
force
you
to
your
Knees.
Your guilt is a mercy,
accept it,
be grateful.

When your soul feels dry,
when it is thirsty and cracking.
Call a woman that you love,
and tell her you love her.
Tell her why,
Tell her how.
Ask her if she needs anything,
Ask her how she is feeling.
Tell her you appreciate her,
Pray for her.

Your light
is bright.
You are beautiful.
In every space that you occupy
you belong where you are comfortable
and where your heart is free.

If you do not feel comfortable
somewhere, leave.
It is not rude,
you are not wrong.
There is no such thing as manners when
your gut is telling you to get out!
I wish my mother had taught me this,
I would have seen so much more of the
world by now.

You are a soul.
Not a body.
Your body will wither and die,
but you,
your essence,
that is infinite.

Notes On Things We've Learned Since
(Space to Record Your Own Lessons):

Preparing My Daughter For Rain

Preparing My Daughter For Rain

What I've learned will not save you
from hurt. It will only show you that
as women we have been made to endure
and grow.
Our bodies are resilient and our souls
are made for a place beyond this.
May HE guide us to the straight path.

Ameen.

Gratitiude:

TB,PB,CB,MB,LQ,CE,KQ,TQ,SQ,SH
RR,RR,AE,AG,TM,NALR,AM
TW,KW,CF,B,J,ST
D,AC,AA,KB
RB,ZI,MJ
CB,AB
KB

Made in the USA
Middletown, DE
07 October 2016